KU-104-894

Pocket Dolly Wisdom

Witty quotes and wise words from Dolly Parton

Dolly's motto:

Dream more,

learn more,

care more

and be more.

Pocket Dolly Wisdom

Witty quotes and wise words from Dolly Parton

hardie grant books

MELBOURNE · LONDON

Contents

Dolly Parton on...

Glamour & Fashion

"People say I look so happy —
and I say,
'That's the Botox.'"

"I wear make-up,
and it gets a little bit
thicker every year."

"I had nothing growing up,
but I always wanted to be
'sexy', even before I knew
what the word was."

"If I have one more
facelift I'll have a beard!"

"I've only had one husband but with all the nips and tucks and plastic surgery I've had he swears he's been with at least three wives."

"It costs a lot of money
to look this cheap."

"I would never stoop so low as to be fashionable."

"I describe my look
as a blend of Mother
Goose, Cinderella, and
the local hooker!"

"I look just like the girl
next door... If you happen
to live next door to an
amusement park."

"I have tennis shoes with little rhinestones that I slip on if I exercise."

"I'm no natural beauty.
If I'm gonna have any looks
at all, I'm gonna have
to create them."

"I always wear heels, even around the house. I'm such a short little thing, I can't reach my kitchen cabinets."

"It's a good thing I was born a girl, otherwise I'd be a drag queen."

"The only way I'd be caught without make-up is if my radio fell in the bathtub while I was taking a bath and electrocuted me... I hope my husband would slap a little lipstick on me before he took me to the morgue."

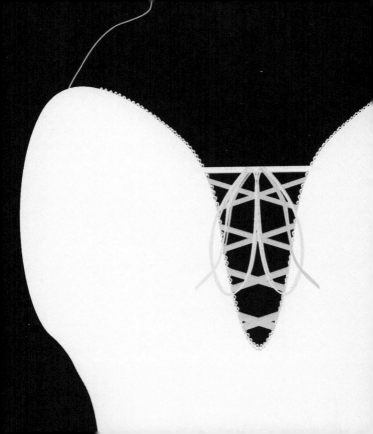

Dolly Parton on...

Her Womanly Assets

"These are my weapons of mass distraction."

"I have little feet because
nothing grows in the shade."

"I'm in showbiz. I look at
my boobs like they're show
horses or show dogs. You've
got to keep 'em groomed."

"My boobs are fake, my hair's fake but what is real is my voice and my heart."

"If I see something sagging, bagging or dragging I'll get it nipped, tucked or sucked."

"Plastic surgeons are always making mountains out of molehills."

"That I can look totally
artificial and be totally real
is perfectly fine with me."

"I was the first woman
to burn my bra — it took
the fire department four
days to put it out."

"My breasts have served me well. I don't know if I'm supporting them or they're supporting me."

"Hey, you try wagging these puppies around a while and see if you don't have back problems."

Dolly Parton on...

Herself

"I know some of the best
Dolly Parton jokes.
I made 'em up myself."

"I'm not offended by all the
dumb blonde jokes because
I know I'm not dumb — and
I'm not blonde either."

"Sometimes my mouth is a little too big and a little too open and sounds too much like a sailor."

"I call myself the
'Dolly Lama', because
people are always
asking my advice."

"A lot of people have said I'd have probably done better in my career if I hadn't looked so cheap and gaudy [but] you shouldn't be blamed because you want to look pretty."

Herself

"It's like what I always say:
I may look fake but I'm real
where it counts."

Dolly Parton on...

Her Successful Career

"I don't kiss nobody's butt."

"Showbusiness is a money-making joke and I've always enjoyed making jokes."

"Writing's just as natural
to me as getting up and
cooking breakfast."

"I'm gonna be making records anyway, even if I had to sell 'em out of the trunk of my car. I'm that kind of musician and singer."

"I'm old enough and cranky enough now that if someone tried to tell me what to do, I'd tell them where to put it."

"I have always been a firm believer in working hard for what is right and for making your own breaks if you want things to change."

"I know who I am; I know
what I can and can't do.
I know what I will and won't
do. I know what I am capable
of and I don't agree to do
things that I don't think
I can pull off."

"I had to get rich so I
could afford to sing like
I was poor again."

"Above everything else
I've done, I've always said
I've had more guts than
I've got talent."

"I look like a woman but
I think like a man. I've done
business with men who think
I'm as silly as I look. By the
time they realise I'm not,
I've done got the money
and gone."

"My songs are like my children — I expect them to support me when I'm old."

"I will never retire unless I had to. As long as I'm able to get up in the morning, get that make-up on, get those high heels on."

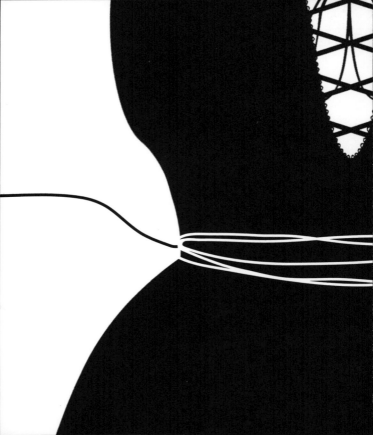

Dolly Parton on...

Diet

"I'm on a seafood diet.
I see food, I eat it."

Diet

"I tried every diet in the
book. I tried some that
weren't in the book.
I tried eating the book.
It tasted better than
most of the diets."

"My weaknesses have
always been food and men
— in that order."

"Every single diet I ever
fell off of was because
of potatoes and gravy
of some sort."

"If I can get my dress on,
my weight is under control."

"I've done everything
every fat person ever has.
I've tried every diet."

Dolly Parton
on...

*Her
Hair*

"I think God gave me talent cos he screwed up my hair."

"Home is where I
hang my hair."

"Someone once asked me,
'How long does it take to
do your hair?' I said, 'I don't
know, I'm never there.'"

"When I was with Andy Warhol, I thought, 'God, his wig looks cheaper than mine!'"

Dolly Parton on...

Men

"When I talk to a man,
I can always tell what he's
thinking by where he's
looking. If he's looking at
my eyes, he's looking for
intelligence. If he's looking
at my mouth, he's looking for
wisdom. If he's looking
anywhere else except my
chest, he's looking for
another man."

"I love to flirt, and I've never
met a man I didn't like."

"I think women are
beautiful... but I'm
a guy's gal."

"After Momma gave birth to 12 of us kids, we put her up on a pedestal. It was mostly to keep Daddy away from her."

"People are always asking me in interviews, 'What do you think of foreign affairs?' I just say, 'I've had a few.'"

"I've been accused of being
involved with every man
I'm ever seen with. Maybe
I have, maybe I ain't.
I never tell if I have."

Dolly Parton on...

Love

"When someone shows
you their true colours,
believe them."

"Yes, I support gay marriage.
They have every right
to be as miserable as
straight people."

"I'll never harden my heart,
but I've toughened the
muscles around it."

"I'm one of those people that
if it's something to eat I'm
going to eat the whole thing,
If I'm going to be in love I'm
going to love you all the way
and if my heart's broken, it's
just shattered all to pieces."

"The secret to a long marriage is to stay gone."

"I think everyone should
be with who they love."

Dolly Parton on...

Life

"The way I see it, if you want
the rainbow, you gotta put
up with the rain!"

"Find out who you are
and do it on purpose."

"Don't get so busy making
a living that you forget to
make a life."

"Storms make trees
take deeper roots."

"Some days, they pan out a little better than others, but you still gotta always just try."

"My philosophy is simple:
it's a down-home,
common, horse-sense
approach to things."

"If you see someone without a smile, give them yours."

"You never do a whole lot unless you're brave enough to try."

Pocket Dolly Wisdom

First published in 2014 by Hardie Grant Books

Hardie Grant Books (UK)
5th & 6th Floors
52-54 Southwark Street
London SE1 1RU
www.hardiegrant.co.uk

Hardie Grant Books (Australia)
Ground Floor, Building 1
658 Church Street
Melbourne, VIC 3121
www.hardiegrant.com.au

All rights reserved. No part of this publication may be reproduced,
stored in a retrieval system or transmitted in any form by any
means, electronic, electrostatic, magnetic tape, mechanical,
photocopying, recording or otherwise, without
the prior written permission of the Publisher.

British Library Cataloguing-in-Publication Data. A catalogue record
for this book is available from the British Library.

ISBN: 978-1-78488-001-9

Publisher: Kate Pollard
Senior Editor: Kajal Mistry
Art Direction: Emilia Toia
Front cover illustration © Kayci Wheatley, www.kayciwheatley.com
Back cover illustration © Posteritty, www.posteritty.com
Illustrations on pages iv, 16, 28-9, 50-1, 58-9, 80-81 © Posteritty
Illustrations on pages ii, vi, 64-5, 72-3 © Shutterstock
Colour Reproduction by p2d

Printed and bound in China by 1010

10 9 8 7 6 5 4 3 2 1